COUNTRIES

D0178672

Portugal

Alice Harman

Explore the world with Popcorn - your complete first non-fiction library.

Look out for more titles in the Popcorn range. All books have the same format of simple text and striking images. Text is carefully matched to the pictures to help readers to identify and understand key vocabulary. www.waylandbooks.co.uk/popcorn

Published in paperback in 2013 by Wayland
Copyright © Wayland 2013

Wayland
Hachette Children's Books
338 Euston Road
London NW1 3BH

Wayland Australia
Level 17/207 Kent Street
Sydney NSW 2000

Produced for Wayland by
White-Thomson Publishing Ltd
www.wtpub.co.uk
+44 (0)843 208 7460

Editor: Alice Harman
Designer: Clare Nicholas
Picture researcher: Alice Harman
Series consultant: Kate Ruttle
Design concept: Paul Cherrill

British Library Cataloging in Publication Data
Harman, Alice. 1987-
   Portugal. -- (Countries)(Popcorn)
   1. Portugal--Juvenile literature.
   I. Title II. Series
   914.6'9-dc23

ISBN: 978 0 7502 7921 5

10 9 8 7 6 5 4 3 2 1

Wayland is a division of Hachette Children's Books,
an Hachette UK company.
www.hachette.co.uk

Printed and bound in Malaysia

Picture/Illustration Credits: Alamy: John Warburton-Lee 6, Travelshots.com 15, Kuttig-Travel 16, Robert Estall 17; Peter Bull: 23; Stefan Chabluk: 4; Dreamstime: Andrea Haase 7, Devy 11, Phillippehalle 12, Jmarijs 13, Luis Santos 16(t), Rui Matos 20, Homydesign 21 (and imprint); iStock: arssecreta 14; Shutterstock: devi title page and 8, Rui Ferreira 9, rubiphoto 10, fstockfoto 18, Rui Alexandre Araujo 19; Travel Library: John Lawrence front cover; Wikimedia: fulviusbsas 5

Every effort has been made to clear copyright. Should there be any inadvertent omission, please apply to the publisher for rectification.

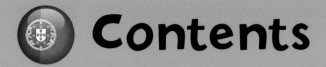# Contents

Where is Portugal?

Here is a map of Portugal. Portugal is in southwest Europe. It is next to Spain.

Braga

Cantabrian Mountains

Porto

River Douro

Coimbra

Atlantic Ocean

Serra da Estrela

PORTUGAL

SPAIN

River Tagus

Sintra

Lisbon

Évora

River Guadiana

Beja

EUROPE

ALGARVE

Sagres

Faro

Lisbon is the capital of Portugal. It is by the coast. There is a castle on the tallest hill above the city.

Lisbon is further west than any other European capital.

Some parts of St. George's Castle are 1,500 years old.

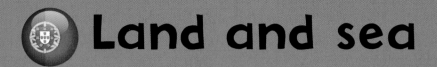 Land and sea

The north of Portugal has many hills and mountains. There are lots of forests. In the south, the land is flatter and there are fewer trees.

In the north, grapes are grown on terraces on the sides of hills.

Portugal has a long coast.
The coast faces the Atlantic
Ocean. There are sandy and
stony beaches.

The steep, rocky cliffs along the coast
are often orange and white striped.

cliff

The weather

Most of Portugal is warm in the summer. It is hotter and drier in the south.

In summer, the Algarve region is the hottest place in Europe.

Millions of tourists come to Portugal every year to enjoy the sunny beaches.

In winter, it is still quite warm in most of the country. There is a lot more rain, especially in northern Portugal. It sometimes snows in the mountains.

Serra da Estrela is the highest mountain range in Portugal. Many people ski here in winter.

Town and country

You can find old buildings and narrow streets in the centre of most towns. Just outside the centre, there are modern houses and wide, busy roads.

Bairro Alto is one of the oldest places in Lisbon.

Portugal has many small farms in the countryside. Farmers often grow olives or tomatoes.

Some farmers still use animals, not machines such as tractors, to work on their farms.

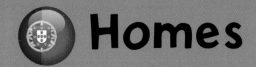 Homes

The city of Porto is famous for its old, colourful houses. Some of these houses are decorated with coloured ceramic tiles called azulejos.

These houses in Porto are usually split up into three or four smaller flats.

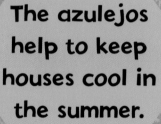

The azulejos help to keep houses cool in the summer.

On the Portuguese island of Madeira, there are traditional triangle-shaped country houses. The steep, wide roofs are made of straw.

These houses are always painted red, white and blue.

13

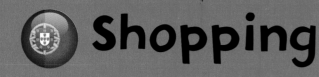 # Shopping

Portugal has modern shopping malls and supermarkets where people buy food, clothes and other goods. There are also shops along the city streets.

Rua Augusta, the main shopping street in Lisbon, has a famous stone arch at one end.

arch

Portugal has many markets in its villages, towns and cities. Most markets sell food grown and made by local people.

This stall in Sintra town market sells meats and cheeses.

 Food

There are lots of cafés in Portugal.
People often go there to drink
coffee or fruit juice, and eat
sweet pastries.

Cafés in the city are often
very old and beautiful. This
café is over 100 years old.

These are famous
Portuguese pastries,
called 'nata.'

People in Portugal eat lots of fresh fish. The country has a long coast, and many people go fishing in the sea.

People in Portugal eat more fish than in any other country in Europe.

This fisherman is selling the fish he caught just a few hours earlier.

 Sport

Football is the most popular sport in Portugal. Portuguese football teams often win European competitions such as the UEFA Cup.

Cristiano Ronaldo is a famous Portuguese football player.

Many people in Portugal enjoy cycling and watching bicycle races. The 'Volta a Portugal' is a famous long-distance race.

People racing in the 'Volta a Portugal' cycle more than 1500km, and ride up and down many mountains.

Holidays and festivals

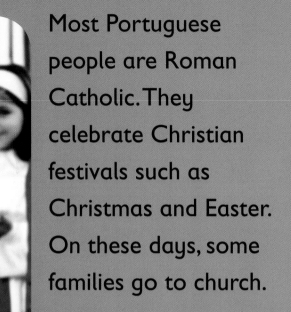

Most Portuguese people are Roman Catholic. They celebrate Christian festivals such as Christmas and Easter. On these days, some families go to church.

Colours have special meanings in the Church. At Easter, purple means sadness and white means joy.

Carnival is a day in February or March when there are huge street parties all over Portugal. People dress up, dance and have fun together.

The town of Ovar in Portugal is famous for having the biggest and craziest Carnival!

Countries such as Brazil and Italy also celebrate Carnival.

Speak Portuguese!

Olá! *(o-la)* — Hello

Adeus! *(ad-ay-oosh)* — Goodbye

Sim *(sing)* — Yes

Não *(now)* — No

Por favor *(por fav-or)* — Please

Obrigado *(ob-ree-gar-do)* — Thank you (if you're a boy, say this)

Obrigada *(ob-ree-gar-da)* — Thank you (if you're a girl, say this)

O meu nome é *(o may-oo nom-ee ay)* — My name is

Como vai? *(com vy)* — How are you?

The green of the flag means hope. The red means courage.

Make an azulejo

Azulejos are coloured ceramic tiles, typical of Portugal. They cover the fronts of some houses in Porto.

1. Take a handful of clay and mix it with a few drops of water, to soften it. Using the rolling pin, roll the clay out on a flat, smooth surface. Don't make it too thin.

2. Use the plastic knife to cut a square out of the flattened clay. Use a ruler to help you. Pull the extra clay away from the edges of the square.

3. Leave the clay square to dry flat on a wire rack for 24–48 hours, in a cool and dry place. When your tile is hard, paint it with colourful patterns.

Glossary

capital the city where the government of the country meets

ceramic clay cooked in a very hot oven so it becomes hard

joy a feeling of great happiness

olive a small green or black fruit that is eaten and used to make cooking oil

region an area of a country

Roman Catholic a Christian whose spiritual leader is the Pope in Rome

skiing a winter sport in which people slide down snowy mountains

terraces wide, flat steps cut into the lower slopes of hills or mountains

tiles flat pieces of baked clay placed in rows to cover floors, walls and roofs

tourist someone who travels for fun or on holiday

Index

24